THE SMART START RN WORKBOOK

THE **SMART** START RN WORKBOOK

Practical Tools for

Money Decisions That Compound for Decades

Companion to ***The Smart Start RN*** (RN Wealth Series –Book 1)

Steve R. Reckons, RN, MPA, BS Finance

GAMS
RELEVANCE
PRESS

An imprint of GAMS Relevance, LLC

COPYRIGHT PAGE

Disclaimer: This workbook is for educational purposes only and does not provide financial, legal, tax, medical, or professional advice. You are responsible for your decisions and outcomes. Consider consulting qualified professionals for guidance specific to your situation.

During production, AI-assisted tools were used to draft worksheet tables, standardize templates, and create basic line diagrams for clarity. All concepts, structure, and final editorial decisions represent the author's intent and judgment.

ISBN:978-1-972505-01-4

Published by
GAMS Relevance Press
An imprint of GAMS Relevance, LLC
Oklahoma City, Oklahoma
Printed in the United States of America

First Edition

For bulk orders, speaking inquiries, or institutional partnerships:
hello@gamsrelevance.com

HOW TO USE THIS WORKBOOK

This workbook is meant to reduce pressure, not add another obligation.

Use it like triage:

1. Identify the pressure source.
2. Make the smallest repeatable move.
3. Review quarterly.
4. Set a review date

You do not need to complete every page. You need to complete the pages that match your current reality.

Rule: If a page makes you feel worse, you are using it wrong. Pick a smaller move.

FORMAT NOTE

The Kindle version is designed for reading and reference.

This workbook is best used in print if you prefer writing directly on the pages.

COMPANION NOTE

This workbook is the implementation companion to ***The Smart Start RN***.

- If you want the framework—how debt, lifestyle, and investing choices compound across a nursing career—start with ***The Smart Start RN***.

- If you already read it, this workbook is the next step: worksheets, decision rules, scripts, and a quarterly maintenance protocol built for real schedules.

The goal is not intensity. The goal is structure—so stability does not depend on constant overtime, permanent night work, or peak capacity that never changes.

READER NOTE

If you want this workbook to work, don't use it as a burst of motivation. Use it as a maintenance practice.

- Do one worksheet when pressure rises.

- Use decision rules when you feel behind.

- Use scripts to reduce avoidance.

- Use the quarterly review to prevent drift.

Time rewards stability.

NAVIGATION MAP (START HERE) ➧

If your main problem **is debt pressure:**
Start with **Section B — Chapter 2 Worksheet (Financial Triage + Debt Containment)** → then **Section C3** → then **Section E.**

If your main problem is **night shift trap or fatigue spending:**
Start with **Section B — Chapter 3 Worksheet (Night Shift Triage + Baseline Freeze)** → then **Section D7** → then **Section C2.**

If your main problem **is investing avoidance or panic:**
Start with **Section B — Chapter 4 Worksheet (Investing Defaults)** → then **Section C4** → then **Section D6.**

If your main problem **is job mismatch or burnout risk:**
Start with **Section B — Chapter 5 Worksheet (Job Leverage + True Pay)** → then **Section E6** → then **Section C5.**

If you are in **disruption mode right now:**
Start with **Section C6 (If Life Blows Up)** → then return to **Section A.**

RED FLAG INDEX (SYMPTOMS → TOOL)

If you're not sure where to start, start with the symptom you recognize most. Then use the tool listed. Don't optimize. Don't do five things. Do one.

If this is your symptom… → Start here

- **Overtime feels required to stay afloat → B2 Financial Triage + Debt Containment**, then **C3 Debt Containment Setup**, then **D2 Overtime Rule**
- **You're using credit for normal life → B2 Financial Triage + Debt Containment**, then **C1 System Stabilizer**, then **C2 Micro-Buffer Setup**
- **Night shift differential is supporting your baseline → B3 Night Shift Triage**, then **D7 Baseline Freeze Rule**, then **C2 Micro-Buffer Setup**
- **Convenience/fatigue spending is rising → B3 Night Shift Triage (Fatigue Spending section)**, then **D7 Baseline Freeze Rule**
- **You haven't started investing (or it's inconsistent) → B4 Investing Defaults**, then **C4 Investing Defaults Setup**, then **D5 Investing Rule**
- **You feel behind and want to take a risky shortcut → D6 Catch-Up Rule**, then **B6 Timeline Reality Check**
- **A job change is on the table → B5 Job Leverage + True Pay**, then **E6 Recruiter/Manager Leverage Script**, then **C5 Job Leverage Setup**
- **Life blew up (income hit, illness, family event) → C6 If Life Blows Up**, then restart with **A5 7 Days (Stabilize)**

Minimum rule: If you can't finish the full tool, complete only the **Action** line and set a **Next review date**.

WHAT THIS WORKBOOK IS — AND IS NOT

This workbook is:

- A practical tool set: worksheets, checklists, decision rules, scripts, and quarterly reviews
- Designed for nursing schedules and variable capacity
- Built to reduce drift and preserve flexibility over time

This workbook is not:

- A budgeting planner that requires daily tracking
- A stock-picking or "beat the market" guide
- A promise of fast results

If you want faster results through intensity, this will feel slow. If you want stability that survives real life, this will fit.

WHAT CHANGES IF YOU USE THIS

If this system holds, here is what shifts over time:

- Overtime becomes optional, not required
- Fixed costs become manageable on baseline pay
- Investing continues without constant attention
- You can reduce effort temporarily without financial panic
- Job decisions become less fragile

THE SMART START RN MODEL (IN 90 SECONDS)

This workbook is built around one idea: most nurses don't struggle because they lack income. They struggle because early decisions quietly harden into permanence.

The three loads that shape your future:

1. **Debt load** — payments that dictate your schedule
2. **Lifestyle load** — fixed costs that assume overtime or differential pay
3. **Investing defaults** — whether compounding is automatic or delayed

The constraint most plans ignore: capacity.
A plan that depends on peak energy is not a plan. It's a temporary performance.

The goal is not intensity. The goal is structure.
So stability does not depend on constant overtime, permanent night work, or peak capacity that never changes.

What "progress" looks like in this model:

- Overtime becomes optional, not required
- Fixed costs become manageable on baseline pay
- Investing becomes boring and automatic
- You can reduce effort temporarily without financial panic
- Job decisions become less fragile

If you can build that, time will do work you cannot force through willpower.

SECTION A QUICK START LADDER

Introduction

This section is designed to get you moving without turning your finances into a second job. The goal is not to "get caught up" overnight. The goal is to stabilize your system and reduce pressure with small, repeatable moves. If you can do three durable things in the next week, you are already ahead of the pattern that traps most nurses: intensity followed by burnout.

A1. How To Use This Workbook (10 Minutes, Not A Lifestyle)

This workbook is not meant to become another obligation. It is meant to reduce pressure.

Use it like triage:

- Identify the pressure source.
- Make the smallest repeatable adjustment.
- Stop. Let time do work.

Rule: If a page makes you feel worse, you are using it wrong. Pick a smaller move.

Best use: 20 minutes once per week for 4 weeks.
Minimum use: 10 minutes today, then one page per month.

A2. Stable / Strained / Exposed (What This Means)

Circle the one that fits *right now*. You can change categories without failing.

STABLE

- Overtime is optional, not required.
- Most surprises are absorbable without credit.
- Your plan still works in an average month.

STRAINED

- You're staying current, but it takes effort.
- A schedule change would create immediate stress.
- You may be borrowing energy to stay afloat.

EXPOSED

- One disruption would force credit, missed payments, or panic.
- Debt and fixed obligations are dictating your schedule.
- You can't reduce hours without consequences.

Today I am: ☐ Stable ☐ Strained ☐ Exposed
Why (one line): ____

If you only have 10 minutes, complete A3 and schedule your first tool.

A3. Find Your Starting Point in 5 Minutes

You do not need to fix everything. You need to pick the right first pressure.

1) Circle the primary pressure source

☐ Debt payments (a "schedule enforcer")

☐ Night shift trap / fatigue spending

☐ Fixed costs too high

☐ Investing not started (or inconsistent)

☐ Job mismatch (pay is high but recovery is bad)

☐ Life disruption (divorce, illness, move, family responsibilities)

☐ Other: ______________________________

2) What does the pressure cause? (check all that apply)

☐ Overtime feels required

☐ Sleep and recovery are failing

☐ You're using credit for normal life

☐ You avoid looking because it feels heavy

☐ You keep "resetting" but not building

☐ You feel behind and tempted to take risky shortcuts

3) Pick ONE tool to use first

☐ Financial Triage (Chapter 2 tool)

☐ Night Shift Triage (Chapter 3 tool)

☐ Job Leverage (Chapter 5 tool)

☐ Checklist: Stabilize the System

☐ Checklist: Debt Containment

☐ Checklist: Investing Defaults

☐ "If life blows up" protocol

My first tool is: ______________________________

Date I will do it (within 72 hours): ______________

A4. Your Status Today + One Pressure Source (10 Minutes)

Today I am: ☐ Stable ☐ Strained ☐ Exposed

My one pressure source is: ______________________________

If I reduced this pressure by 10%, what changes first?

☐ Less overtime dependency

☐ Better sleep / less fatigue spending

☐ Fewer "surprise" expenses turning into credit

☐ More consistent investing

☐ More job flexibility

☐ Less dread

The smallest repeatable move I can do this week is:

☐ One call (APR / hardship / due date change)

☐ One freeze (no new fixed costs for 30 days)

☐ One cap (fatigue spending cap for 14 days)

☐ One automation (micro-buffer or investing)

☐ One comparison (Job Leverage scorecard)

☐ One cancellation/downsizing decision

My smallest move: ____
When I will do it: ____

A5. The Ladder — 7 Days (Stabilize)

These are not goals. They are stabilizers.

Complete at least 3 of 5.

1. ☐ List your fixed obligations + minimum debt payments (one page, rough numbers)
2. ☐ Put minimums on autopay OR set calendar reminders for top 3 bills
3. ☐ Start a micro-buffer: $____ per paycheck (even $25 counts)
4. ☐ Freeze new fixed costs for 30 days (subscriptions, upgrades, new payments)
5. ☐ Pick one fatigue-spend category and cap it for 14 days: ____________ at $____ / week

What changed in 7 days (one line):

____

Status after 7 days: ☐ Stable ☐ Strained ☐ Exposed

Next step: ☐ Move to 30 Days ☐ Repeat 7 Days

A6. The Ladder — 30 Days (Contain)

Containment means the system works without heroic effort.

Complete at least 3 of 5.

1. ☐ Identify your **schedule enforcer** payment (the one that forces overtime)
2. ☐ Make one containment move (call, refinance, negotiate, sell-down plan, term change)
3. ☐ Convert one relief spend into recovery (plan + boundary): ____________________
4. ☐ Capture match OR set investing default (auto): $____ or ____% per paycheck
5. ☐ Score your current job with the Job Leverage tool (or score an offer)

What changed in 30 days (one line):

____

Status after 30 days: ☐ Stable ☐ Strained ☐ Exposed

Next step: ☐ Move to 90 Days ☐ Repeat 30 Days

A7. The Ladder — 90 Days (Compound)

Compounding is not intensity. It is consistency.

Complete at least 3 of 5.

1. ☐ Increase investing by 1% or $25/paycheck (only if Stable/Strained—not Exposed)
2. ☐ Build buffer to one month baseline (even partial progress counts)
3. ☐ Remove or reduce one fixed obligation (or cut it by 10%)
4. ☐ "No new financial products for 90 days" rule (protect against panic decisions)
5. ☐ Complete Quarterly Review + Vitals Dashboard

What changed in 90 days (one line):______________________________

Status after 90 days: ☐ Stable ☐ Strained ☐ Exposed

Next step: ☐ Quarterly maintenance ☐ Repeat 90 Days

A8. If You Only Do 3 Things (The Minimum Viable System)

If you do nothing else, do these:

1. **Micro-buffer**: $____ per paycheck
2. **Contain the schedule-enforcer debt** (one action in 2 weeks)
3. **Investing default** (match or $25/paycheck) — boring on purpose

My 3 commitments (fill in):

- Buffer: $____ per paycheck
- Debt action within 14 days: ______________________________
- Investing default: $____ or ____% per paycheck

Date I start: _____________ **Date I review:** _____________

NUMBERS FIELD GUIDE (ESTIMATES, NOT PERFECTION)

If numbers make you freeze, use estimates. The goal is direction, not precision.

1) Monthly take-home (estimate)

- **Weekly pay:** paycheck × 4
- **Biweekly pay:** paycheck × 2
- **Two jobs / variable:** use last month's deposits and round

2) Fixed obligations (what counts)
Count anything that is due whether you feel good or not:

- Rent/mortgage, car, insurance, minimum debt payments, phone, core utilities, childcare
  Do not overthink groceries, gas, or one-offs for this line.

3) Minimum debt payments
Use the total of minimums (not what you *hope* to pay extra).

4) Buffer months
Buffer months = (cash you can access) ÷ (core monthly expenses)
If you don't know core expenses, estimate it from the last month and round.

5) Fatigue spending
You're not tracking "everything." You're identifying the top 1–3 categories that rise when you're exhausted:

- delivery/fast food, convenience stores, rides/parking, impulse spending, subscriptions added in hard months

Rule: If you can't estimate a number in 60 seconds, write "unknown" and move forward. The worksheet still works.

SECTION B — WORKSHEETS

Introduction:

These worksheets translate the book's ideas into decisions you can make on an average week. They are not meant to be completed perfectly, but honestly. Each worksheet ends with one small action and a review date, because the point is not a one-time breakthrough. The point is creating a structure that keeps working when your schedule gets heavy.

B1. Chapter 1 Worksheet — Capacity & Optionality Map

Purpose: Identify what's consuming capacity and what preserves freedom so your plan doesn't depend on peak energy.

Book 1 concept: *A plan that depends on peak capacity is fragile.*

Intake

Date: ____________

Shift pattern: ☐ Days ☐ Nights ☐ Rotating

This week feels like: ☐ Normal ☐ Heavy ☐ Unsustainable

Sleep quality (0–10): ___ **Money stress (0–10):** ___

Block 1 — Capacity Snapshot (no judgment)

Recovery time available this week: ☐ Low ☐ Medium ☐ High

Cognitive load (0–10): ___

Block 2 — Three Non-Negotiables (baseline stability)

Define what "protected" looks like this month:

- **Housing stability:**

  ____

- **Transportation reliability:** ______________________________
- **Recovery protected (sleep/health):** ________________________

Block 3 — Optionality Check (what breaks first)

If you reduced effort by 20% next month, what breaks first?

☐ Fixed bills ☐ Debt minimums ☐ Food ☐ Childcare ☐ Transportation ☐ Other: __________

Block 4 — Quiet Commitments Audit (what assume peak capacity)

☐ Overtime-as-normal

☐ Lifestyle baseline sized to differential

☐ Subscriptions you "won't touch"

☐ Payment(s) that trigger anxiety

☐ A plan that only works in an ideal week

One commitment I will keep temporary on purpose:

____

Review date: ____________

Action

Choose one:

☐ Auto-transfer to buffer ($**/paycheck)**

☐ **Autopay one bill / due-date cleanup**

☐ **Spending cap for one fatigue category ($**/week)

☐ "No new fixed obligations" for 30 days

☐ 10-minute weekly review day (day): ____________

I will do this by (date): ____________

Status: Stable / Strained / Exposed
Next review date: ____________
If this is not done by the date above, reduce the scope—not the intention.

Notes: ____

B2. Chapter 2 Worksheet — Financial Triage + Debt Containment Planner

Purpose: Identify pressure points, assess flexibility, and contain "schedule-enforcer" debt so money stops dictating your schedule.

Book 1 concept: *If a payment forces overtime, it isn't manageable.*

Intake

Date: ____________

Pay schedule: ☐ Weekly ☐ Biweekly ☐ Other: __________

Shift pattern: ☐ Days ☐ Nights ☐ Rotating
Avg hours/week: ______
Money stress (0–10): ___

Overtime required to feel stable? ☐ Yes ☐ No ☐ Sometimes

Block 1 — Financial Vitals (rough numbers are fine)

Take-home per month (estimate): $__________
Fixed obligations per month (estimate): $__________
Minimum debt payments per month: $__________

Fixed-cost load feels like: ☐ Light ☐ Manageable ☐ Heavy ☐ Crushing

Emergency buffer (months of core expenses): ☐ 0 ☐ <1 ☐ 1–3 ☐ 3–6 ☐ 6+

Use credit for normal life sometimes? ☐ Yes ☐ No ☐ Recently

Block 2 — Exposure (what is doing the squeezing)

☐ Lifestyle assumes overtime rescue

☐ Debt limits ability to reduce hours

☐ Plan depends on peak capacity (energy/health/schedule)

☐ A schedule change would create immediate stress

☐ Avoidance is increasing because it feels heavy

☐ Stable only when nothing goes wrong

Primary exposure (one line):

____

Block 3 — Flexibility Check (60–90 days)

If you reduced effort by 20% for one month, would you stay current on minimums?
☐ Yes ☐ No ☐ Unsure

In 60–90 days, could you:

☐ Say no to overtime ☐ Absorb a normal surprise ☐ Reduce hours ☐ Change shifts/units ☐ Take unpaid time off

Biggest constraint to flexibility:

____

Block 4 — Debt Containment (integrated)

Debt is contained when it no longer dictates behavior.

Payment stress test

1. Skip overtime for one month → stay current on minimums? ☐ Yes ☐ No ☐ Unsure
2. Income drop 10% for 60 days → need credit? ☐ Yes ☐ No ☐ Unsure

Schedule Enforcers (top 3 payments that force overtime/differentials)

Payment	Monthly	Rate (if known)	Why it enforces behavior
1	$____	____%	______________________________
2	$____	____%	______________________________
3	$____	____%	______________________________

#1 schedule enforcer: ______________________ ($____/mo)

Contained definition (one sentence):
"This payment is contained when
____."

Action — Containment Move (choose one path + date)

Circle one:

☐ Refinance / rate reduction

☐ Term change (temporary relief)

☐ Hardship / modification

☐ Balance transfer plan (with end date)

☐ Sell / downsize (car/housing/expense)

☐ Freeze new charges + stabilize

☐ Other: _________________________

One decision I will make in the next 14 days:

____

Decision date (within 14 days): ____________

Status: Stable / Strained / Exposed
Next review date: ____________
If this is not done by the date above, reduce the scope—not the intention.

Notes: ____

B3. Chapter 3 Worksheet — Night Shift Financial Triage + Fatigue Spending & Baseline Freeze

Purpose: Prevent the night differential from becoming a permanent baseline and convert fatigue spending into recovery and stability.

Book 1 concept: *Temporary pay should not fund permanent baseline.*

Intake

Date: ____________

Shift pattern: ☐ Nights ☐ Rotating ☐ Days (former nights)

Time on nights: ☐ <6 mo ☐ 6–12 mo ☐ 1–3 yrs ☐ 3+ yrs

Money stress (0–10): ___ **Sleep quality (0–10):** ___

Block 1 — Income vs Recovery Assumptions

☐ Continued differential ☐ Frequent overtime ☐ Short recovery time

☐ High tolerance for disruption ☐ "I'll fix this later"

Most fragile assumption:

____

Day-shift test: If nights ended in 60–90 days, could you cover core expenses on day pay?

☐ Yes ☐ No ☐ Unsure

Core expenses (monthly): $__________

Minimum debt payments (monthly): $__________

Buffer (months): ☐ 0 ☐ <1 ☐ 1–3 ☐ 3–6 ☐ 6+

Block 2 — Exposure (what nights are holding up)

☐ Lifestyle assumes night income

☐ Convenience spending rising

☐ Recovery worsening → spending increases

☐ Plan depends on energy you're borrowing

☐ I don't know my baseline without nights

Primary exposure (one line):

____

Block 3 — Fatigue Spending Map (last 14 days)

1. ______________________________ approx $____/week
2. ______________________________ approx $____/week
3. ______________________________ approx $____/week

Primary trigger: ☐ Short staffing ☐ Poor sleep ☐ Schedule flip ☐ Stress ☐ Back-to-back ☐ Other: ________

Block 4 — Relief vs Recovery (convert one leak)

Pick your #1 category: ______________________________

Most of this is: ☐ Relief ☐ Recovery ☐ Mixed

Convert $____/week from relief → recovery by doing:

My 14-day rule:

"When I feel the trigger, I will ___________________ instead of ___________________."

Action — Baseline Freeze (30 days)

For 30 days, I will not add:

☐ New subscription ☐ New payment ☐ New recurring service ☐ Upgrade tied to differential

One enjoyment expense I keep on purpose: ____________________
Cap: $____/month

One move I will make this week:

____

I will do it by (date): ___________

Status: Stable / Strained / Exposed
Next review date: ___________
If this is not done by the date above, reduce the scope—not the intention.

Notes: ____

B4. Chapter 4 Worksheet — Investing Defaults Setup

Purpose: Make investing "participation," not research—set defaults you can keep in hard months.

Book 1 concept: *Boring defaults beat perfect timing.*

Intake

Date: ____________

Employer plan available? ☐ Yes ☐ No ☐ Unknown

Block 1 — Match Capture (baseline compensation)

If match exists: **% needed:** ___% **My current %:** ___%

☐ Increase to capture full match by next pay date: ____________

☐ Not offered / not eligible / unsure

Block 2 — Contribution Default (sustainable)

☐ $____ per paycheck ☐ ____% per paycheck

Start date: ____________

Block 3 — Investment Default (boring on purpose)

☐ Target-date fund ☐ Broad index fund ☐ Other:

____

1-minute explanation test: ☐ Pass ☐ Fail (If fail, simplify.)

Block 4 — Fee/Complexity Screen (quick)

Expense ratio/fees (if known): ____% ☐ Unknown (I will check once)

Red flags:

☐ I don't understand the product

☐ Fees feel complicated

☐ It's exciting/story-driven

☐ I feel urgency to "catch up"

Action

My investing default is: ____________________ at ☐ $____ ☐ ____% per paycheck
I will set/confirm it by (date): ____________

Status: Stable / Strained / Exposed
Next review date: ____________
If this is not done by the date above, reduce the scope—not the intention.

Notes: ____

B5. Chapter 5 Worksheet — Job Leverage Scorecard + True Pay + Offer Comparator

Purpose: Evaluate jobs as systems—pay, recovery, staffing reality—so headline pay doesn't quietly cost flexibility.

Book 1 concept: *Recovery is part of compensation.*

Intake

Date: ____________

Evaluating: ☐ Current job ☐ Offer A vs B ☐ Potential transfer/unit change

Block 1 — Job Leverage Scorecard (1–5 each)

1 = fragile / staffing-dependent
3 = workable but exposed
5 = stable / recovery-friendly

1. Schedule predictability ___
2. Unit strain & staffing reality ___
3. Recovery friendliness ___
4. Benefit package quality ___
5. Skill portability & growth path ___
6. Internal mobility & support ___
7. Commute & friction costs ___
8. Pay structure quality ___

Total (out of 40): ________
Interpretation: 32–40 High leverage | 24–31 Mixed | 16–23 Staffing-dependent | 8–15 Fragile

Block 2 — True Pay (quick estimate)

Add: retirement match +$____ | usable PTO +$____
Subtract: health out-of-pocket −$____ | commute/friction −$____

True Pay estimate (annual): $___________

Block 3 — Offer Comparator (if comparing)

Job A: ___________________ **Job B:** ___________________
True Pay A: $_________ **True Pay B:** $_________

Recovery cost (after 3 consecutive shifts):

- Job A: ☐ Functional ☐ Depleted ☐ Wrecked
- Job B: ☐ Functional ☐ Depleted ☐ Wrecked

Convenience-spending risk (fatigue tax):

- Job A: ☐ Low ☐ Medium ☐ High
- Job B: ☐ Low ☐ Medium ☐ High

Dealbreakers (check any):

☐ Mandatory overtime ☐ Unstable rotation ☐ Chronic short staffing

☐ Weak benefits/PTO ☐ Poor portability ☐ Commute/friction heavy

Action

Decision sentence: "I'm choosing _________________ because it preserves _________________."
I will act/decide by (date): ___________

Status: Stable / Strained / Exposed

Next review date: ___________

If this is not done by the date above, reduce the scope—not the intention.

Notes: ____

B6. Chapter 6 Worksheet — Timeline Reality Check

Purpose: Turn the "millionaire timeline" into stability metrics and guardrails that prevent panic decisions.

Book 1 concept: *Consistency compounds; urgency usually sabotages it.*

Intake

Date: ____________ **Years in nursing:** ______

Progress feels: ☐ Invisible ☐ Slow ☐ Uneven ☐ Encouraging

Block 1 — Visibility Trap

What I expected to feel by now:

____

Block 2 — The milestone that matters (check what's true)

☐ Overtime not required for normal surprises

☐ Investing continues during busy periods

☐ Career decisions feel less fragile

☐ Buffer absorbs a normal hit

☐ Plan doesn't require constant attention

If only one is true, which one?

____

Block 3 — Impatience Triggers (risk behaviors)

When I feel behind, I'm tempted to:

☐ Stock pick ☐ Risky products ☐ Overwork ☐ Abandon plan ☐ Big lifestyle upgrade

Action

My guardrail: "When behind-feeling rises, I do nothing new for 7 days."
Next review date: ____________

Status: Stable / Strained / Exposed
Next review date: ____________
If this is not done by the date above, reduce the scope—not the intention.

Notes: ____

B7. Chapter 7 Worksheet — Future-Self Protection Plan

Purpose: Translate older-nurse hindsight into one protective action that preserves future capacity and flexibility.

Book 1 concept: *Early decisions harden into permanence unless you make them temporary on purpose.*

Intake

Date: ___________

10 years from now I want:

____

Block 1 — Assumptions that could harden (pick 3)

☐ "I'll always tolerate nights."

☐ "I can always work more."

☐ "This payment is temporary."

☐ "I'll invest later."

☐ "Recovery will stay easy."

☐ Other: ____________________

Block 2 — Make one thing temporary on purpose

Decision drifting toward permanence:

____

Make it temporary with a review date: ___________

Block 3 — One kindness to future capacity (pick one)

☐ Reduce/renegotiate one fixed obligation

☐ Automate one protective action (buffer/investing)

☐ Build a transition skill (cert/role exposure/portfolio)

☐ Protect a recovery boundary (sleep day/no extra shift rule)

Action

Action I will take before next review:

____

I will do it by (date): ______________

Status: Stable / Strained / Exposed
Next review date: ______________

If this is not done by the date above, reduce the scope—not the intention.

Notes: ____

SECTION C — ONE-TIME SETUP CHECKLISTS

Introduction:
These checklists are the "set it once" parts of your financial system. They reduce late fees, reduce mental load, and reduce the need for overtime to rescue routine problems. Most financial stress is not caused by lack of intelligence. It is caused by fragile systems: due dates that don't match paydays, payments that depend on perfect weeks, and decisions that never get made because they feel too big. This section turns those into a short sequence you can complete and then maintain quarterly.

C1. System Stabilizer (Bills, Due Dates, Autopay)

Purpose: Reduce late-fee risk and mental load by making the system run on an average week, not a perfect week.

Book 1 concept: *Stability is often a systems problem, not an income problem.*

Intake

Date: __________

Pay schedule: ☐ Weekly ☐ Biweekly ☐ Other: ______
Overtime currently required? ☐ Yes ☐ No ☐ Sometimes

Block 1 — Bill Map (capture, don't optimize)

Complete what you can in 10 minutes. Rough is fine.

Bill / Obligation	Amount	Due date	Autopay? (Y/N)	Notes
Rent/Mortgage	$____	___	☐Y ☐N	_________
Car	$____	___	☐Y ☐N	_________
Insurance	$____	___	☐Y ☐N	_________
Phone	$____	___	☐Y ☐N	_________
Utilities	$____	___	☐Y ☐N	_________
Minimum debt	$____	___	☐Y ☐N	_________

Block 2 — Due-Date Cleanup (reduce timing risk)

Check all that apply:

☐ Cluster major due dates after payday (where possible)

☐ Move at least one due date to reduce "end-of-month crush"

☐ Set reminders for any bill not on autopay

☐ Remove paper mail surprises (go paperless if helpful)

Bills I will request a due-date change for (up to 2):

1. ____________________ 2) ____________________

Block 3 — Autopay Priority (minimums first)

Autopay order:

1. Housing
2. Transportation
3. Insurance
4. Minimum debt payments
5. Utilities/phone

I will set autopay for (circle one): 1 bill / 2 bills / 3 bills this week

Action

One autopay or due-date change I will complete by (date):

____

Task:

____

Status: Stable / Strained / Exposed
Next review date: ____________
If this is not done by the date above, reduce the scope—not the intention.

Notes: ____

C2. Micro-Buffer Setup (Small Money, Big Stability)

Purpose: Create a buffer that prevents normal surprises from becoming credit or panic.

Book 1 concept: *Small buffers prevent normal life from turning into credit.*

Intake

Date: ____________

Current buffer months: ☐ 0 ☐ <1 ☐ 1–3 ☐ 3–6 ☐ 6+

Block 1 — Choose the smallest repeatable transfer

Pick one:

☐ $10/week

☐ $25/paycheck

☐ $50/paycheck

☐ Other: $____

Where will it go?

☐ Separate savings account

☐ Same bank, separate "buffer" bucket

☐ Cash envelope (temporary)

☐ Other: ____________________

Block 2 — Name the buffer (so you don't steal it)

Buffer name: ☐ "Surprises" ☐ "Stability" ☐ "No-Panic Fund"

☐ Other: ________

Block 3 — Define what it is used for (and what it is not)

Buffer is for:

☐ Car repair ☐ copay/meds ☐ small emergency travel ☐ short income gap ☐ required expense

Buffer is NOT for:

☐ lifestyle upgrades ☐ gifts/holidays ☐ "treats" ☐ new recurring bills

Action

My micro-buffer transfer is: $____ ☐ weekly ☐ per paycheck
Start date: ____________ **Bank/app task I will complete by:** ____________

Status: Stable / Strained / Exposed
Next review date: ____________
If this is not done by the date above, reduce the scope—not the intention.

Notes: ____

C3. Debt Containment Setup (Docs, Calls, Sequence)

Purpose: Contain the "schedule-enforcer" payment with an actionable sequence—so relief is structural, not temporary.

Book 1 concept: *Contain the schedule enforcer before you optimize anything else.*

Intake

Date: ____________
#1 schedule enforcer payment: _____________________ $____/month

Block 1 — Gather what you need (10 minutes)

☐ Account number

☐ Current balance

☐ Interest rate (APR)

☐ Minimum payment

☐ Payoff amount

☐ Term remaining (if loan)

☐ Last 3 statements (optional)

☐ Credit score estimate (optional)

Block 2 — Choose one containment path (circle one)

☐ Refinance / rate reduction

☐ Hardship / modification

☐ Term change (temporary relief)

☐ Balance transfer plan (with end date)

☐ Sell / downsize (car/housing/expense)

☐ Freeze new charges + stabilize

☐ Other: _______________________

Block 3 — Call/Action Sequence (keep it simple)

This week:

☐ Make 1 call using a script

☐ Get 1 written offer/option

☐ Compare 2 options (rate/term/payment)

☐ Decide (do not "keep shopping" indefinitely)

Calls to make (up to 2):

1. ______________________________ Date: _____________
2. ______________________________ Date: _____________

Block 4 — Freeze rule (stop the leak while you contain)

For 30 days:

☐ No new charges on revolving debt

☐ No new "temporary" upgrades

☐ No new recurring payments

Action

My containment decision deadline (within 14 days): _____________
The decision I will make:

____

Status: Stable / Strained / Exposed

Next review date: _____________

If this is not done by the date above, reduce the scope—not the intention.

Notes: ____

C4. Investing Defaults Setup (Match, Default Fund, Auto-Increase)

Purpose: Make investing automatic and boring so it survives hard months.

Book 1 concept: *Participation beats research.*

Intake

Date: ____________

Employer plan? ☐ Yes ☐ No ☐ Unknown

Currently investing? ☐ Yes ☐ No ☐ Inconsistent

Block 1 — Match capture (if offered)

☐ Confirm match details

Match % required for full match: ___%

My current %: ___%

☐ Increase to full match by next pay date: ____________

Block 2 — Set the default contribution

Choose one:

☐ $____ per paycheck

☐ ____% per paycheck

Start date: ____________

Block 3 — Choose the default fund (boring on purpose)

☐ Target-date fund

☐ Broad index fund

☐ Other (must be explainable in 60 seconds): ____________________

Block 4 — Auto-increase (small, safe, consistent)

Choose one:

☐ +1% annually

☐ +$25 per quarter

☐ Other: ____________________

Block 5 — Protective rule (avoid panic products)

☐ "No new financial products for 90 days."

Action

I will set/confirm my investing default by (date): ____________

Default: ____________________ at ☐ $____ ☐ ____% per paycheck

Status: Stable / Strained / Exposed

Next review date: ____________

If this is not done by the date above, reduce the scope—not the intention.

Notes: ____

C5. Job Leverage Setup (Score + One Upgrade Plan)

Purpose: Improve flexibility by improving the job system—not just chasing higher pay.

Book 1 concept: *Better structure beats higher headline pay.*

Intake

Date: ___________

Current role/unit: ___________________________

Schedule type: ☐ Days ☐ Nights ☐ Rotating

Block 1 — Score your current role (fast)

Complete the Job Leverage Scorecard in Section B.

Your score (out of 40): _______

Block 2 — Identify one leverage upgrade

Pick one category to improve in the next 90 days:

☐ Schedule predictability

☐ Staffing strain exposure

☐ Recovery friendliness

☐ Benefits/PTO quality

☐ Skill portability (cert/experience)

☐ Internal mobility/support

☐ Commute/friction

☐ Pay structure quality

Chosen leverage upgrade:

____

Block 3 — Upgrade path (one concrete move)

Choose one:

☐ Talk to manager about schedule/rotation expectations

☐ Apply to a different unit with better recovery

☐ Start/finish a certification pathway

☐ Shadow/observe a role with better leverage

☐ Build an internal transfer plan (timeline + requirements)

Action

One leverage move I will make by (date): ___________

Task:

____

Status: Stable / Strained / Exposed

Next review date: ____________

If this is not done by the date above, reduce the scope—not the intention.

Notes: ____

C6. If Life Blows Up (72-hour Triage Protocol)

Purpose: Prevent disruption from turning into long-term damage. This is stabilization, not optimization.

Book 1 concept: *Triage prevents disruption from becoming long-term damage.*

Intake

Date: ____________ **Disruption:** ______________________________

☐ Income hit ☐ Health event ☐ Family responsibility ☐ Move ☐ Relationship change ☐ Other: ________

Block 1 — Protect the basics first (today)

☐ Housing paid/secured

☐ Transportation maintained

☐ Food basics covered

☐ Minimum payments identified

☐ Medication/health needs covered

Block 2 — Pause what can be paused (24 hours)

☐ Pause extra debt payments (keep minimums)

☐ Stop nonessential spending for 7 days

☐ Pause investing temporarily if truly necessary (restart plan set)

☐ Cancel one optional subscription if cash tight

Block 3 — Communicate early (48 hours)

☐ Call lender/creditor BEFORE you miss a payment (use script)

☐ Ask about hardship options / due date change

☐ Notify HR if schedule/income will change

Block 4 — Restart plan (within 7 days)

☐ Micro-buffer restarted at $____

☐ Investing restarted at ☐ $____ ☐ ____% by date ____________

☐ One containment action scheduled for date ____________

Action

The one thing I will do in the next 24 hours:

____

Support I will ask for (one line):

____

Status: Stable / Strained / Exposed

Next review date: ____________

If this is not done by the date above, reduce the scope—not the intention.

Notes: ____

SECTION D — DECISION-RULE CARDS

Introduction:
When nurses feel behind, the risk is not inactivity. The risk is overreaction: risky products, lifestyle upgrades, or overtime patterns that borrow too much from the body. Decision rules prevent that. They are simple on purpose. They create guardrails so your worst financial decisions are harder to make during your most exhausted weeks.

D1. How to Use Decision Rules

Purpose: Turn good intentions into repeatable behavior by choosing a few rules you will actually follow under stress.

Block 1 — What decision rules are (and are not)

Decision rules are:

☐ Simple

☐ Repeatable

☐ Designed for tired weeks

☐ Stronger than motivation

Decision rules are not:

☐ Detailed plans

☐ A personality test

☐ A way to judge yourself

Block 2 — Choose your top 3 rules (start here)

Pick three rules to use for the next 90 days:

☐ D2 Overtime Rule

☐ D3 Lifestyle Rule

☐ D4 Debt Rule

☐ D5 Investing Rule

☐ D6 Catch-Up Rule

☐ D7 Baseline Freeze Rule

My top 3 rules are:

1. ____________ 2) ____________ 3) ____________

Block 3 — Identify rule breaks (so you can protect against it)

I'm most likely to break rules when:

☐ After a brutal stretch of shifts

☐ When I feel behind or embarrassed

☐ When I'm bored and want a quick win

☐ After a hard personal event

☐ When I get a pay bump or bonus

☐ Other: ____________________

Action

For the next 90 days, my rule is: "When stress spikes, I follow my top 3 rules before I do anything new."
Start date: ____________ **Review date:** ____________

Status: Stable / Strained / Exposed
Next review date: ____________
If this is not done by the date above, reduce the scope—not the intention.

Notes: ____

D2. Overtime Rule Card

Purpose: Prevent overtime from becoming the default solution that keeps the system fragile.

Block 1 — Overtime is allowed only when:

Check all that must be true:

☐ I am sleeping adequately (not in a deficit spiral)

☐ I am not using overtime to cover minimum payments

☐ I am not using overtime to fund a permanent expense

☐ My baseline bills are already manageable

☐ My extra money is for (buffer, containment, investing)

Block 2 — Overtime is forbidden when:

Check any that are true:

☐ I'm doing it out of panic or shame

☐ I'm exhausted enough that spending will spike anyway

☐ I'm already behind on recovery

☐ It's being used to keep an unsustainable payment alive

☐ It's being used to justify a lifestyle upgrade

Action

My overtime purpose (if allowed): ☐ Buffer ☐ Debt containment ☐ Investing ☐ One-time need
Cap for the next 30 days: ____ extra shifts OR ____ extra hours
Review date: ____________

Status: Stable / Strained / Exposed
Next review date: ____________
If this is not done by the date above, reduce the scope—not the intention.

Notes: ____

D3. Lifestyle Rule Card

Purpose: Stop temporary income (differentials, overtime, bonuses) from creating permanent obligations.

Block 1 — The rule (write it once)

No permanent expenses funded by temporary pay.

Block 2 — Permanent expenses to protect against

Check what you will treat as "permanent":

☐ New car payment

☐ New rent/mortgage increase

☐ Subscription bundle

☐ Private school/childcare jump

☐ Large recurring service (meals, deliveries, memberships)

☐ Other: ____________________

Block 3 — The exception clause (keep it narrow)

A permanent expense is allowed only if:

☐ It still works on day-shift pay / no overtime

☐ It does not increase money stress

☐ It does not reduce buffer building

☐ It passes the 60–90 day flexibility test

Action

One permanent expense I will not add for 90 days:

____

Review date: ____________

Status: Stable / Strained / Exposed
Next review date: ____________

D4. Debt Rule Card

Purpose: Identify and contain "schedule-enforcer" debt—the payment that dictates your life.

Block 1 — The rule

If a payment forces overtime, it is not manageable.

Block 2 — Schedule-enforcer test

If I skipped overtime for one month, would I stay current on minimums?
☐ Yes ☐ No ☐ Unsure

If income dropped 10% for 60 days, would I need credit?
☐ Yes ☐ No ☐ Unsure

Block 3 — Containment trigger

If you check "No" or "Unsure" above, then:
☐ I must do Debt Containment (Section B / C) before I make any upgrades.

Action

My schedule-enforcer payment is: ______________________
($_____/month)
My containment action is scheduled for: _____________

Status: Stable / Strained / Exposed
Next review date: _____________
If this is not done by the date above, reduce the scope—not the intention.

Notes: ____

D5. Investing Rule Card

Purpose: Keep investing simple and durable so it survives busy seasons.

Block 1 — The rule

Boring beats perfect. Participation beats research.

Block 2 — The one-minute explanation test

If I can't explain an investment in 60 seconds, I don't buy it.
☐ Agreed ☐ I need to simplify

Block 3 — Default commitment

My default is:

☐ Target-date fund

☐ Broad index fund

☐ Other: ______________________ (must be explainable in one minute)

Action

My investing default is: ______________________

Contribution: ☐ $____/paycheck ☐ ____%
I will set/confirm it by: ____________

Status: Stable / Strained / Exposed
Next review date: ____________
If this is not done by the date above, reduce the scope—not the intention.

Notes: ____

D6. Catch-Up Rule Card

Purpose: Prevent "behind-feeling" from triggering risky decisions.

Block 1 — The rule

When behind-feeling rises, I do nothing new for 7 days.

Block 2 — What counts as "new"

New means:

☐ New investment product

☐ New loan or refinance without containment plan

☐ New recurring bill

☐ A big purchase justified by stress

☐ A dramatic budget reset

Block 3 — What you do instead (during the 7 days)

During the 7 days, I will do one of these:

☐ Micro-buffer transfer

☐ Pay down schedule-enforcer (small extra)

☐ Complete one worksheet page

☐ Make one script call

☐ Sleep/recovery reset plan (reduce fatigue spending)

Action

My 7-day default action is: ______________________________
Start date: ____________ **End date:** ____________

Status: Stable / Strained / Exposed
Next review date: ____________
If this is not done by the date above, reduce the scope—not the intention.

D7. Baseline Freeze Rule Card

Purpose: Stop fatigue and stress from turning into lifestyle creep.

Block 1 — The rule

For 30 days after a hard stretch, no new fixed costs.

Block 2 — What counts as fixed costs

☐ Subscriptions ☐ payments ☐ upgrades ☐ memberships ☐ recurring deliveries ☐ "small" monthly add-ons

Block 3 — The replacement plan (so it's livable)

Pick one:

☐ Keep one enjoyment expense capped at $____/month

☐ Replace delivery with a default plan (groceries/snacks)

☐ Choose a low-friction recovery option: ____________________

Action

My 30-day freeze starts: ____________
My one allowed enjoyment expense (capped): ____________________
$____/month
Review date: ____________

Status: Stable / Strained / Exposed
Next review date: ____________
If this is not done by the date above, reduce the scope—not the intention.

Notes: ____

SECTION E — SCRIPTS

Introduction:
A lot of stability is created through short conversations: lowering an APR, changing a due date, clarifying a benefit, or asking the right questions before you accept a job. The problem is that those conversations are easy to avoid. Scripts remove the guesswork. You do not need to sound impressive. You need to sound calm, direct, and consistent—and then write down the outcome.

E1. Script Guide (How to Use These Without Overthinking)

Purpose: Make one call, ask the right questions, and capture the outcome so progress is real—not emotional.

Block 1 — Your tone (calm, firm, brief)

Use this posture:

- "I want to keep this account in good standing."
- "I'm looking for options available today."
- "Please explain the terms and the end date."

Avoid:

- Overexplaining your life
- Apologizing for asking
- Agreeing to terms you don't understand

Block 2 — Outcome rules (what to record)

After every call, write:

☐ Date/time

☐ Rep name/ID

☐ Offer details (rate/term/payment/end date)

☐ What happens next

☐ When you will follow up

Action

My first script call will be: ☐ APR ☐ Hardship ☐ Due date change ☐ Recruiter questions ☐ Household boundary
I will do it by (date): ___________

Status: Stable / Strained / Exposed
Next review date: ___________
If this is not done by the date above, reduce the scope—not the intention.

Notes: ____

E2. APR Reduction Script (Credit Card)

Purpose: Reduce interest cost and shorten payoff time without adding complexity.

What to say (script)

"Hi, I've been a customer for ___ years. I want to keep the account in good standing, but the APR is too high. Can you reduce my APR or offer a promotional rate? What options are available today?"

If they resist:
"I'm deciding whether to move this balance. If you can lower the rate today, I can keep it here."

What to ask (must-ask questions)

☐ "What is the new APR and when does it start?"

☐ "Is there a promo period? When does it end?"

☐ "Is there a fee?"

☐ "Does this change my minimum payment?"

☐ "Will this affect my account standing?"

Outcome Log

Date/time: ____________ Company: _____________________
Rep name/ID: _____________________
Current APR: ____% New APR / Promo: %
Promo end date (if any): ____________
Fees: ☐ None ☐ Yes: $
Notes on terms:

____

Result: ☐ Approved ☐ Denied ☐ Offered alternative:

____

Action

Next step: ☐ Accept offer ☐ Call back ☐ Compare with another option
Next action date: ___________

Status: Stable / Strained / Exposed
Next review date: ___________
If this is not done by the date above, reduce the scope—not the intention.

Notes: ____

E3. Hardship / Payment Modification Script

Purpose: Prevent missed payments and contain a schedule-enforcer debt before it becomes long-term damage.

What to say (script)

"Hi, I want to keep this account current. My schedule and cash flow have been uneven, and I'm looking for hardship or payment modification options that keep me in good standing. What options are available right now?"

What to ask (must-ask questions)

☐ "Will this be reported as late or delinquent?"
☐ "Does interest continue during the program?"
☐ "What is the new payment and for how long?"
☐ "What happens when the program ends?"
☐ "Are there fees?"
☐ "Do I need to stop using the account?"
☐ "Can you send the terms in writing?"

Outcome Log

Date/time: ____________ **Company:** ____________________
Rep name/ID: ____________________
Offer type: ☐ Reduced payment ☐ Rate reduction ☐ Deferral ☐ Other: ______
New payment: $____ **Duration:** ______ months
Interest continues? ☐ Yes ☐ No ☐ Unknown
Reporting impact: ☐ None ☐ Possible ☐ Unknown
End-of-program terms: ____
Written terms sent? ☐ Yes ☐ No

Result: ☐ Approved ☐ Denied ☐ Follow-up required:

____

Action

Next step: ☐ Accept ☐ Decline ☐ Call back ☐ Compare options
Decision deadline (date): ____________

Status: Stable / Strained / Exposed
Next review date: ____________
If this is not done by the date above, reduce the scope—not the intention.

Notes: ____

E4. Due Date Change + Autopay Setup Script

Purpose: Reduce timing risk by aligning bills with paydays.

What to say (script)

"Hi, I get paid on ___ and ___. I'd like to change my due date to ___ so I can pay on time consistently. What dates are available?"

What to ask

☐ "When will the due date change take effect?"

☐ "Will this create a partial payment or double payment this cycle?"

☐ "Can you confirm the new due date in writing/email?"

☐ "Can I set autopay for the minimum payment?"

Outcome Log

Date/time: ____________ **Company:** _____________________
Rep name/ID: _____________________
Old due date: ______ **New due date:** ______
Effective date: ______

One-time adjustment needed? ☐ No ☐ Yes: _____________________

Autopay set? ☐ Yes ☐ No ☐ Not available

Action

Next step I will complete by (date): ____________
Task:

____

Status: Stable / Strained / Exposed
Next review date: _____________
If this is not done by the date above, reduce the scope—not the intention.

Notes: ____

E5. Collections / Settlement Boundary Script (What NOT to Say)

Purpose: Keep you from accidentally agreeing to terms that worsen your position.

What to say (script)

"I'm calling to understand what options exist. I'm not agreeing to anything today. Please provide the offer and terms in writing."

If pressured: "I'm not able to commit on this call. I will review written terms and respond."

What to ask

☐ "Please confirm the total balance and any fees."

☐ "Is this offer time-limited? What is the deadline?"

☐ "Will you provide the terms in writing?"

☐ "If I pay, how will it be reported?"

☐ "Is the debt validated/documented?"

Do NOT say (protective boundaries)

☐ Don't admit fault or make emotional statements

☐ Don't agree to "small payments today" without terms

☐ Don't provide new bank access details if you're unsure

☐ Don't accept anything you don't understand

Outcome Log

Date/time: ____________ **Company:** ____________________
Rep name/ID: ____________________
Offer summary:

____

Written terms requested: ☐ Yes ☐ No
Deadline given: ____________

Action

Next step: ☐ Wait for written terms ☐ Consult advisor ☐ Compare options
Review date: ____________

Status: Stable / Strained / Exposed
Next review date: ____________
If this is not done by the date above, reduce the scope—not the intention.

Notes: ____

E6. Recruiter / Manager Leverage Script + Question List

Purpose: Prevent headline pay from masking poor recovery, unstable staffing, or schedule risk.

What to say (script)

"I'm comparing roles based on recovery, staffing reality, and schedule predictability—not just base pay. Can I ask a few direct questions?"

Questions (ask the ones that matter most)

Staffing reality

☐ "How often are nurses floated?"

☐ "How often is mandatory overtime used?"

☐ "What is the typical assignment on a hard night?"

☐ "What happens when the unit is short?"

Schedule predictability

☐ "What does weekend requirement mean in practice?"

☐ "How far in advance is the schedule posted?"

☐ "How often do shifts get changed?"

Recovery + orientation

☐ "How long is orientation and is it protected?"

☐ "What is the culture around breaks?"

☐ "What is turnover like in the last year?"

Pay structure

☐ "What differentials apply and when?"

☐ "Are raises standardized or discretionary?"

☐ "What is the benefit cost per paycheck?"

Notes Page (use during the call)

Role/Unit: ____________________ **Facility:** ____________________
Red flags noticed (one line): ____________________________________
Best sign noticed (one line): ____________________________________

Action

I will score this role using the Job Leverage worksheet by (date):

____

Status: Stable / Strained / Exposed
Next review date: ____________
If this is not done by the date above, reduce the scope—not the intention.

Notes: ____

E7. Household Boundary Script (Baseline Freeze / Overtime Boundary)

Purpose: Create shared expectations so stability does not depend on constant extra shifts.

What to say (script)

"I'm building a plan that doesn't require overtime to survive. For the next 30 days, we're freezing new fixed expenses and capping fatigue spending at $____ per week. This is to protect long-term flexibility. After 30 days, we'll review what changed."

If there's resistance:
"This is not punishment. This is a stability move. We can adjust after we see the results."

What to agree on (check all that apply)

☐ No new subscriptions/payments for 30 days

☐ One enjoyment expense allowed, capped at $____/month

☐ Overtime only for: ☐ buffer ☐ containment ☐ one-time need

☐ Weekly 10-minute review day: ____________

Outcome Log (after the conversation)

Date: ____________
Agreements made:

____

One boundary that matters most:

____

Review date: ____________

Action

I will start the 30-day freeze on (date): ____________
I will review outcomes on (date): ____________

Status: Stable / Strained / Exposed
Next review date: ____________
If this is not done by the date above, reduce the scope—not the intention.

Notes: ____

SECTION F — CASE STUDIES: CHOOSE-YOUR-MOVE PATHWAYS

Introduction:

Case studies are here to reduce hesitation. Many nurses know what they "should" do, but they don't trust the sequence. Each case shows two paths: the wrong move that feels right in the moment, and the durable move that protects future flexibility. The goal is not to judge the wrong move. The goal is to recognize it quickly and choose a better pattern next time.

F1. Case Study 1 — New Grad + Car Note + Credit Card

Purpose: Show how "manageable payments" become schedule-enforcers—and how to contain them without shame or heroics.

Snapshot (what's happening)

You're a new nurse. Income is real for the first time. You financed a car because reliability matters. You used a credit card for a few "start-up" expenses—then life kept happening. Now minimum payments are steady, but breathing room is thin.

Primary pressure source (circle one):
Debt payments / Fixed costs / Overtime dependency / Behind-feeling

Most accurate status today: Stable / Strained / Exposed

The wrong move that feels right (Path A)

"I'll fix this by working more."

- Add overtime as the default solution
- Make minimums, maybe pay a little extra
- Keep spending patterns mostly unchanged
- Tell yourself it's temporary

What happens next (typical outcome):

- Exhaustion rises → fatigue spending rises
- Overtime becomes required, not optional
- Investing gets delayed
- A single disruption (sick week, family need) triggers credit use

The durable move (Path B)

Contain the schedule-enforcer first.

- Identify the payment that dictates your schedule
- Use a containment path (rate reduction, term change, sell/downsize, hardship options)
- Freeze new charges while you contain
- Start a micro-buffer so "normal surprises" stop hitting the card

What happens next (typical outcome):

- Pressure drops before income rises
- Overtime becomes optional again
- You can start investing with boring defaults
- One disruption is annoying—not catastrophic

Choose-Your-Move (circle one)

I'm choosing: ☐ Path A (more work) ☐ Path B (containment)

Do This Worksheet Now

Minimum viable completion: If you can't do the full worksheet, complete only the **Action** line and set the **Next review date**.

☐ Section B: Chapter 2 Worksheet — Financial Triage + Debt Containment

Then: ☐ **Section C3 — Debt Containment Setup** and ☐ **Section C2 — Micro-Buffer Setup**

30-Day Follow-Up Plan

One containment action scheduled by (date): ____________

Micro-buffer started at: $____ ☐ weekly ☐ per paycheck

Rule for 30 days: ☐ No new charges ☐ No new fixed costs

Status: Stable / Strained / Exposed

Next review date: ____________

If this is not done by the date above, reduce the scope—not the intention.

Notes: ____

F2. Case Study 2 — Night Shift Differential + Lifestyle Creep

Purpose: Show how the night differential quietly becomes a permanent baseline—and how to stop the trap without deprivation.

Snapshot (what's happening)

Nights pay more. Nights also take more. At first, the differential feels like progress. Over time, recovery gets harder. Convenience spending rises. Then the lifestyle begins to assume the differential. The trap is not nights. The trap is building a baseline that requires nights forever.

Primary pressure source (circle one):
Night shift trap / Fatigue spending / Fixed costs / Recovery failure

Most accurate status today: Stable / Strained / Exposed

The wrong move that feels right (Path A)

"I deserve this. Nights are hard."

- Small upgrades become normal
- Subscriptions accumulate
- Delivery and convenience become recovery substitutes
- Differential becomes the invisible funding source

What happens next (typical outcome):

- You can't step down to days without pain
- Overtime gets layered on top
- Investing is inconsistent
- Money stress stays high despite higher pay

The durable move (Path B)

Baseline freeze + relief-to-recovery conversion.

- Freeze new fixed costs for 30 days
- Identify fatigue spending and convert one leak into a recovery plan
- Keep one enjoyment expense capped (so it's livable)
- Run the day-shift test: "could I survive without the differential?"

What happens next (typical outcome):

- Recovery improves
- Convenience spending falls
- The differential becomes a tool—not a requirement
- Days becomes an option again

Choose-Your-Move (circle one)

I'm choosing: ☐ Path A (normalize creep) ☐ Path B (freeze + convert)

Do This Worksheet Now

Minimum viable completion: If you can't do the full worksheet, complete only the **Action** line and set the **Next review date**.

☐ **Section B: Chapter 3 Worksheet — Night Shift Triage + Fatigue Spending + Baseline Freeze**

Then: ☐ **Decision Rule D7 — Baseline Freeze Rule Card** (start date: ________)

30-Day Follow-Up Plan

30-day freeze start date: ____________
One fatigue-spend category to cap: ____________________ at $____/week
One recovery substitution plan:
____

Status: Stable / Strained / Exposed
Next review date: ____________
If this is not done by the date above, reduce the scope—not the intention.

Notes: ____

F3. Case Study 3 — "Behind at 30" Investing Panic

Purpose: Show how behind-feeling triggers risky moves—and how defaults and guardrails create real compounding.

Snapshot (what's happening)

You feel late. You compare yourself to people who started earlier (or who sound confident). You want a fast fix. You're tempted by "strategies," hot funds, crypto chatter, or complex products. The danger is not investing. The danger is investing under stress without guardrails.

Primary pressure source (circle one):
Behind-feeling / Investing inconsistency / Risk-taking impulse

Most accurate status today: Stable / Strained / Exposed

The wrong move that feels right (Path A)

"I need to catch up fast."

- Choose exciting products
- Increase contributions aggressively in a way you can't sustain
- Make frequent changes
- Chase returns to close the gap

What happens next (typical outcome):

- Anxiety stays high
- You quit after a busy season
- You sell at the wrong time
- You lose the one thing that matters: consistency

The durable move (Path B)

Defaults + slow increases + the 7-day rule.

- Set investing default (target-date or broad index)
- Choose a contribution you can maintain during hard months
- Add auto-increase (small, scheduled)
- When behind-feeling spikes: do nothing new for 7 days

What happens next (typical outcome):

- Investing becomes automatic
- You stop "shopping" for salvation
- Your plan survives exhaustion and life events
- Time finally has room to work

Choose-Your-Move (circle one)

I'm choosing: ☐ Path A (fast catch-up) ☐ Path B (defaults + guardrails)

Do This Worksheet Now

Minimum viable completion: If you can't do the full worksheet, complete only the **Action** line and set the **Next review date**.

☐ **Section B: Chapter 4 Worksheet — Investing Defaults Setup**

Then: ☐ **Section C4 — Investing Defaults Setup Checklist**

Also: ☐ **Decision Rule D6 — Catch-Up Rule Card** (start date: _______)

30-Day Follow-Up Plan

Default contribution set at: ☐ $____/paycheck ☐ ____%

Default fund choice: ☐ Target-date ☐ Broad index
Auto-increase plan: ______________________ starting _____________

Status: Stable / Strained / Exposed
Next review date: _____________
If this is not done by the date above, reduce the scope—not the intention.

Notes: ____

F4. Case Study 4 — Higher Pay Offer With Worse Recovery

Purpose: Show how headline pay can hide staffing strain and recovery costs—and how to choose leverage over short-term validation.

Snapshot (what's happening)

You're offered higher pay. Maybe a sign-on bonus. The unit is busy. The schedule is less predictable. You tell yourself you can tolerate it for a year. The hidden cost is recovery. If recovery fails, spending rises, investing becomes inconsistent, and the job starts dictating your life.

Primary pressure source (circle one):
Job mismatch / Recovery cost / Headline-pay bias

Most accurate status today: Stable / Strained / Exposed

The wrong move that feels right (Path A)

"More money solves it."

- Accept the role for pay
- Underestimate staffing strain
- Normalize fatigue spending and overtime
- Tell yourself you'll "fix it later"

What happens next (typical outcome):

- Recovery breaks down
- Spending rises to compensate
- Money stress stays high despite higher income
- You lose flexibility because you're too tired to plan an exit

The durable move (Path B)

Score leverage + true pay + recovery cost before you decide.

- Use Job Leverage Scorecard
- Estimate True Pay (benefits, PTO, commute, health costs)
- Compare recovery cost (functional vs depleted vs wrecked)
- Choose the job that preserves flexibility

What happens next (typical outcome):

- Less burnout risk
- Better consistency with investing and spending
- More optionality (transfers, certifications, role changes)
- Money becomes quieter—not louder

Choose-Your-Move (circle one)

I'm choosing: ☐ Path A (headline pay) ☐ Path B (leverage + recovery)

Do This Worksheet Now

Minimum viable completion: If you can't do the full worksheet, complete only the **Action** line and set the **Next review date**.

☐ **Section B: Chapter 5 Worksheet — Job Leverage + True Pay + Offer Comparator**

Then: ☐ **Script E6 — Recruiter/Manager Leverage Questions**

30-Day Follow-Up Plan

Decision deadline (date): ____________

My decision sentence: "I'm choosing __________________ because it preserves _________________."

One leverage upgrade I will pursue regardless:

____

Status: Stable / Strained / Exposed

Next review date: ____________

If this is not done by the date above, reduce the scope—not the intention.

SECTION G — MAINTENANCE PROTOCOL

Introduction:

Financial stability isn't a finish line—it's maintenance. This section gives you a simple quarterly rhythm to prevent drift: check your vitals, note what changed, make one adjustment. If you can hold the system through busy seasons, time starts doing the heavy lifting.

Completion Ledger (Keep It Real)

This is not a habit tracker, it's your decisions log. If you use this workbook for a year, it shows your system is changing.

Date	Tools Used (A -G)	One Action Taken	Next Review Date
________	_______	______________________________	________
________	_______	______________________________	________
________	_______	______________________________	________
________	_______	______________________________	________
________	_______	______________________________	________
________	_______	______________________________	________
________	_______	______________________________	________

Rule: If you miss a month, restart with one line—not a reset fantasy.

G1. Quarterly Review — Intake

Purpose: Create a calm, repeatable check-in that prevents drift and forces one decision per quarter.

Intake

Quarter: ☐ Q1 ☐ Q2 ☐ Q3 ☐ Q4 **Year:** ______
Date completed: ___________
Today I am: ☐ Stable ☐ Strained ☐ Exposed
Why (one line):

____

Block 1 — What changed since last quarter?

Check all that apply:

☐ Income changed (raise, hours, differential, job change)

☐ Expenses changed (rent, car, childcare, insurance)

☐ Debt changed (new debt, payoff progress, rate change)

☐ Health/recovery changed (sleep, burnout, illness)

☐ Family responsibilities changed

☐ Schedule changed (days/nights/rotation)

☐ Other: _____________________

The biggest change (one line):

____

Action

I will complete my vitals (G2) today and make one decision (G3) by (date): ___________

Status: Stable / Strained / Exposed
Next review date: ___________
If this is not done by the date above, reduce the scope—not the intention.

G2. Financial Vitals Dashboard (Quarterly)

Purpose: Track what actually predicts stability—buffer, fixed-cost load, overtime dependence, and consistency.

Block 1 — Core Vitals (fill rough numbers)

1) Buffer (months of core expenses): ☐ 0 ☐ <1 ☐ 1–3 ☐ 3–6 ☐ 6+

2) Fixed-cost load feels like: ☐ Light ☐ Manageable ☐ Heavy ☐ Crushing

3) Minimum debt payments/month: $__________

4) Overtime required for normal life: ☐ Yes ☐ No ☐ Sometimes

5) Investing status: ☐ On (automatic) ☐ On (manual) ☐ Off ☐ Inconsistent

6) Credit use for normal life: ☐ No ☐ Sometimes ☐ Often

7) Recovery status: ☐ Functional ☐ Depleted ☐ Wrecked

Block 2 — Pass/Fail Stability Tests

Test A: Skip overtime for one month → stay current on minimums?
☐ Pass ☐ Fail ☐ Unsure

Test B: Income drop 10% for 60 days → need credit?
☐ Pass ☐ Fail ☐ Unsure

Test C: Nights ended in 60–90 days → core expenses still manageable?
☐ Pass ☐ Fail ☐ Unsure ☐ Not applicable

Block 3 — Trend Notes (one line each)

What improved this quarter:

____

What worsened this quarter:

____

What stayed fragile:

____

Action

One vital I will improve next quarter: ☐ Buffer ☐ Debt containment ☐ Fixed costs ☐ Investing consistency ☐ Recovery
How I will improve it (one line):

____

Status: Stable / Strained / Exposed
Next review date: ___________
If this is not done by the date above, reduce the scope—not the intention.

Notes: ____

G3. Keep / Cut / Contain / Compound (One Decision Per Quarter)

Purpose: Turn the review into action without turning it into a project.

Block 1 — KEEP (what is working)

List up to 2 things that are working and should be protected:

1. ______________________________
2. ______________________________

Block 2 — CUT (what is quietly weakening you)

List one thing to reduce, cancel, or stop:
Cut: ______________________________
Why: ______________________________

Block 3 — CONTAIN (what dictates your schedule)

Identify one schedule-enforcer or fragile obligation to contain:
Contain: ______________________________ ($____/month if known)

Containment path: ☐ Rate reduction ☐ Term change ☐ Hardship ☐ Sell/downsize ☐ Freeze + stabilize ☐ Other: ______

Block 4 — COMPOUND (what to keep automatic)

Choose one compounding action to keep boring and consistent:

☐ Investing default stays on

☐ Auto-increase (small)

☐ Micro-buffer continues

☐ One leverage upgrade step (job/cert/path)

Action (the only required output)

My one decision this quarter is: ☐ Keep ☐ Cut ☐ Contain ☐ Compound

Decision detail (one sentence):

____

I will complete it by (date): ___________

Status: Stable / Strained / Exposed

Next review date: ___________

If this is not done by the date above, reduce the scope—not the intention.

Notes: ____

G4. 90-Day Reset Page (Tie-back to the Ladder)

Purpose: Restart the system after drift without shame, intensity, or fantasy planning.

Block 1 — Pick your current rung

Right now, I need:

☐ 7 Days (Stabilize)

☐ 30 Days (Contain)

☐ 90 Days (Compound)

Block 2 — Choose 3 moves (minimum viable reset)

Pick three:

☐ Micro-buffer: $____/paycheck

☐ No new fixed costs for 30 days

☐ Containment call scheduled

☐ Investing default set/confirmed

☐ Fatigue-spend cap set

☐ Job leverage score + one upgrade step

☐ Due-date cleanup for 1 bill

My 3 moves are:

1. ______________________ 2) ______________________ 3) ______________________

Block 3 — What caused drift? (so it doesn't repeat)

Drift came from:

☐ Schedule intensity ☐ life event ☐ burnout ☐ avoidance ☐ new payment ☐ lifestyle creep ☐ anxiety investing ☐ other: ________

One protection I add next quarter:

____

Action

Start date: ____________ **Review date (90 days):** ____________

If I miss a week, I will restart with one page—not quit. ☐ Yes

Status: Stable / Strained / Exposed

Next review date: ____________

If this is not done by the date above, reduce the scope—not the intention.

Notes: ____

G5. Quick Quarterly Closeout (One Page)

Purpose: End the quarter with clarity—what you did, what worked, and what you will not do next quarter.

Block 1 — What I completed

One thing I finished:

____

Block 2 — What actually helped

The most helpful change was:

____

Block 3 — What I will not do next quarter

Check any that apply:

☐ Add new fixed costs

☐ Use overtime to keep an unsustainable payment alive

☐ Buy a new investing product under stress

☐ Ignore recovery and call it discipline

☐ Delay decisions until they become crises

Action

My next quarter starts with (circle one): Keep / Cut / Contain / Compound

Next review date: _____________

Status: Stable / Strained / Exposed

Next review date: _____________

If this is not done by the date above, reduce the scope—not the intention.

Notes: ____

ENDING NOTE

You do not need a perfect plan. You need a plan that survives real life. Most nurses don't struggle because they are careless or incapable. They struggle because the system is fragile. Due dates don't match paydays. Payments assume overtime. Recovery is treated like an afterthought. And when pressure rises, the instinct is to fix it with intensity—more shifts, more complexity, more risk.

This workbook is built for the opposite approach. Small moves. Clear guardrails. Boring defaults. Decisions that protect future capacity.

If you complete one worksheet and make one adjustment, you have done something meaningful. If you repeat that quarterly, you've built something rare: a financial system that does not require you to stay at peak output forever.

Your goal isn't to become a different person. Your goal is to reduce the number of ways life can break you. Over time, that changes everything.

Final reminder: When you feel behind, do not rush. Do the next small thing. Then let time do work.

ABOUT THE AUTHOR

Steve R. Reckons is a registered nurse who holds a **B.S. in Finance** and an **MPA**, with **15 years of banking experience** spanning financial specialist and compliance work. After entering nursing, he focused on the gap between standard financial advice and the reality of shift work—fatigue, variable capacity, and institutional pressure. His work emphasizes durable systems: containing debt that dictates behavior, reducing reliance on overtime and differentials, and building simple investing defaults that remain consistent through hard seasons.

ABOUT GAMS RELEVANCE PRESS

GAMS Relevance Press is an imprint of **GAMS Relevance, LLC**.

We publish practical, pressure-tested guides built for real working conditions—especially in healthcare—where time, energy, and recovery are limited. Our focus is durability: clear frameworks, repeatable tools, and decisions that hold up under stress.

PUBLISHER UPDATES & INQUIRIES

GAMS Relevance Press is an imprint of GAMS Relevance, LLC.
For new releases, publisher updates, media rights and inquiries:
GAMSRelevance.com
hello@GAMSRelevance.com

NEXT BOOKS (WHEN YOU'RE READY)

This workbook is designed to help you stabilize early—so your finances don't depend on constant overtime, permanent night work, or perfect months.

Book 1 reminder: If you haven't read **Book 1 — *The Smart Start RN*** yet, start there first. It explains the framework behind these tools and how early decisions around debt, lifestyle load, and investing quietly compound across a nursing career. This workbook is the implementation companion. Book 1 is the foundation.

If you've worked through the tools here and you're noticing a specific shift, that's a good sign. It usually means your problem is no longer "getting started." It's the next constraint.

If your next problem is surplus leakage and slow drift

If you're earning well but flexibility isn't increasing—because surplus is leaking through fixed costs, convenience spending, and "quiet upgrades"—move to:

Book 2 — *Stalled at Six Figures*
How Nurses Turn Income Into Actual Wealth
The RN Wealth Series — Book 2

Book 2 focuses on converting income into retained flexibility—not just higher spending—so your money actually starts doing work.

If your next problem is burnout, capacity, and exit planning

If your income is stable but your capacity is not—if you're thinking about reducing shifts, changing roles, or building a path out of burnout without financial collapse—move to:

Book 3 — *Exit Vitals Stable*
A Financial Path Out of Burnout for Nurses
The RN Wealth Series — Book 3

Book 3 is about protecting recovery and optionality in the later phases—so stepping down, pivoting, or exiting becomes a structured choice, not a crisis response.

You don't need to rush. Use these next books when the constraints change. The goal is the same across every phase: stability that remains durable as your schedule, tolerance, and priorities evolve.

REVIEW REQUEST

If this workbook helped you make calmer, more durable decisions, an honest review helps other nurses find it. Thank you for supporting work built for real schedules.

Notes:

Made in the USA
Monee, IL
04 November 2026

67381897R00056